ORIGAMI FUN

Contents

Dolls

1. Fold a square piece of paper (Fig. 1) so that the edge of AB extends over as far as the center line AC as shown in Fig. 2.

2. Do the same with AD in order to get Fig. 3.

3. Fold along MN so that point C is over and above points B and D. See Fig. 4.

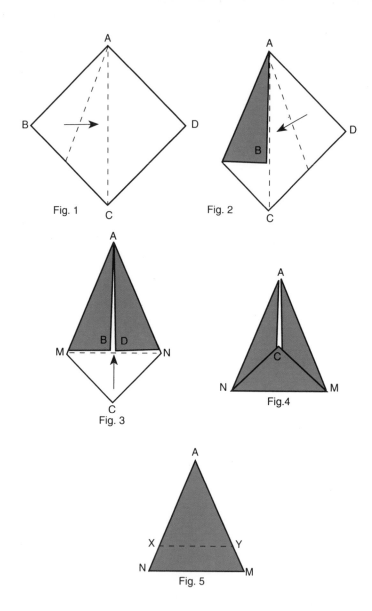

Fig. 1

Fig. 2

Fig. 3

Fig.4

Fig. 5

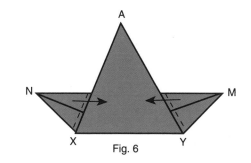

Fig. 6

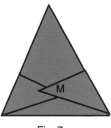

Fig. 7

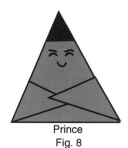

Prince
Fig. 8

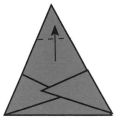

Fig. 9

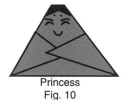

Princess
Fig. 10

4. Turn the paper over and fold back MN along XY about one-third of the way up (Fig. 5) to get Fig.6.

5. Fold points M and N forward along AY and AX so as to overlap each other as in Fig. 7.

6. Complete the doll by drawing the face (Fig. 8).

7. To make a princess (Fig. 10), fold back the top of the head as shown in Fig. 9.

Clown

1. Fold a square piece of paper along lines DE and DF (Fig. 1) so that edges BD and CD meet at the center AD (Fig. 2).

2. Cut MN and PO approximately 3/4 of the way to the center (Fig. 2).

3. Fold along AN and AO (Fig. 3) so that the two side flaps overlap each other (Fig. 4).

4. Cut slit XY about the length of NO and slightly less than half an inch below EF (Fig. 4).

5. Fold along EF (Fig. 4), bring point A forward and through slit XY (Fig. 5).

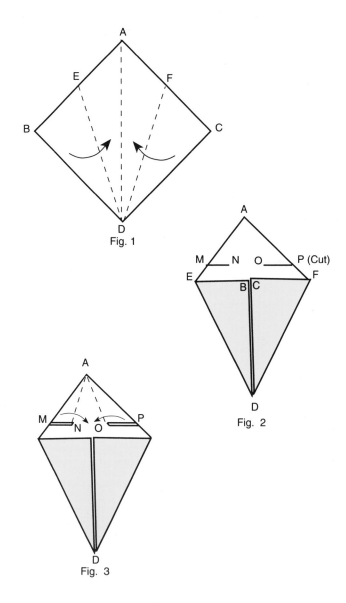

Fig. 1

Fig. 2

Fig. 3

4

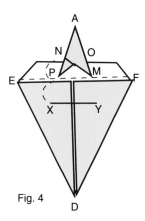

Fig. 4

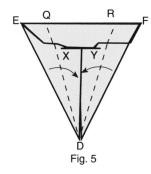

Fig. 5

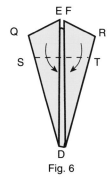

Fig. 6

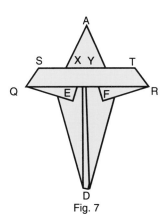

Fig. 7

6. Fold along QD and RD (Fig. 5) so that points E and F meet at the center (Fig. 6).

7. Fold along ST (Fig. 6), bringing QR forward, and point A will come up by itself (Fig. 7). Line ST is on XY.

8. To make the legs, cut the lower part of AD from D (Fig. 7).

9. Turn the paper over and draw the face.

Crane

1. Fold a square piece of paper at line BC so that point A is over point D (Figs. 1 & 2).

2. Fold at ED so that point B is over point C (Fig. 3).

3. As shown in Figs. 3 and 4, open B and bring it over until it is directly above D. Crease paper along EF and EG.

4. Turn it over and you will have Fig. 5. Do the same with C as you did with B and the result is Fig. 6.

5. Crease at YC and ZC (Fig. 7) so that points H and I meet along line EC, and then unfold.

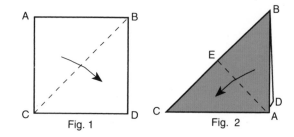

Fig. 1

Fig. 2

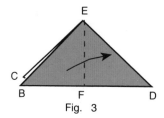

Fig. 3

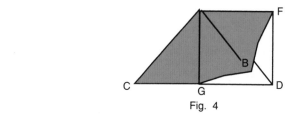

Fig. 4

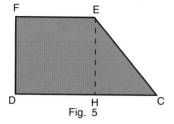

Fig. 5

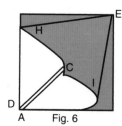

Fig. 6

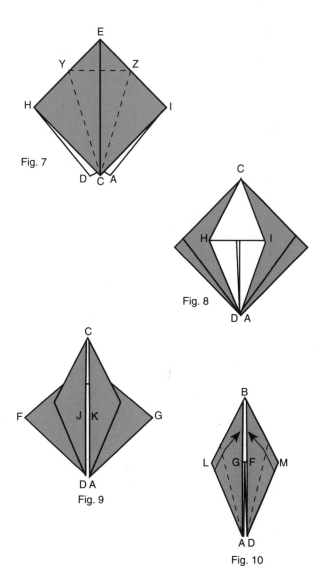

Fig. 7

Fig. 8

Fig. 9

Fig. 10

6. Lift up C and fold at YZ so that H and I meet at the middle along line AC. Fig. 8 shows this step being executed and Fig. 9 shows the completion.

7. Turn the paper over and repeat steps 5 and 6. Resulting in Fig. 10.

8. Fold on the dotted line shown in Fig. 10 so that L and M meet at the middle along lines BA and BD (Fig. 11).

9. Turn the paper over and fold J and K the same way you did L and M. The result is shown in Fig. 12.

10. Lift A up toward the right as shown in Fig. 13 and fold at K. In doing so reverse the fold down the middle of this flap, forming the neck.

11. Next make the head and then fold D to the left to make the tail. Head, neck, and tail are made in the same way as those of the swan.

12. To complete, spread the wings (C and B) open and blow through the hole indicated in Fig. 14 in order to swell out the body.

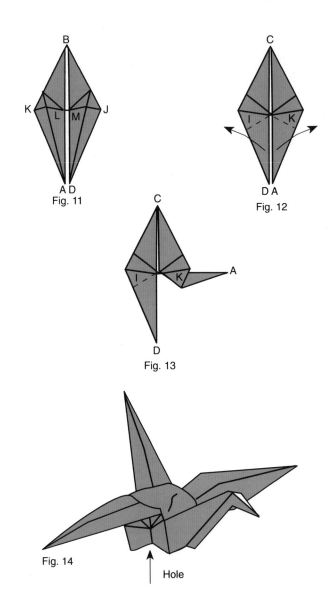

Fig. 11

Fig. 12

Fig. 13

Fig. 14

Hole

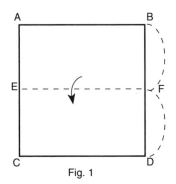

Fig. 1

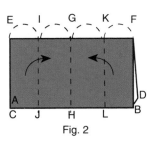

Fig. 2

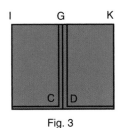

Fig. 3

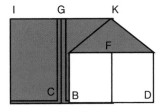

Fig. 4

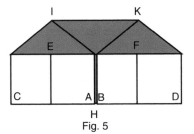

Fig. 5

House

1. Fold a square piece of paper at EF (Fig. 1) so that edge AB is on top of edge CD as in Fig. 2.

2. Fold the edges AEC and BFD forward so that they meet at the center line GH as shown in Fig. 3.

3. Separate points B and D by holding B in place and swinging point D over to the right, thus bringing point F to the position shown in Fig.4.

4. Do the same with points ECA (swinging C to the left) and you will have the paper house shown in Fig. 5.

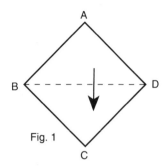

Fig. 1

Candy Box

1. Fold a square piece of paper along line BD (Fig.1) so that corner A falls on corner C (Fig. 2).

2. Fold along EA (Fig 2) so that corner D falls on B (Fig. 3).

3. Open corner D (Fig. 3) and bring it over to the right until it is directly above A (Fig. 4). Then crease along EF and EG (Fig. 5).

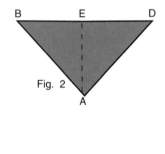

Fig. 2

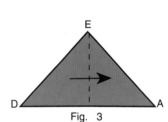

Fig. 3

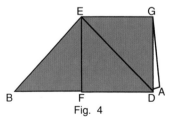

Fig. 4

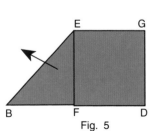

Fig. 5

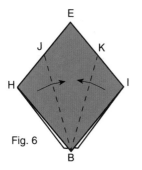

Fig. 6

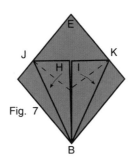

Fig. 7

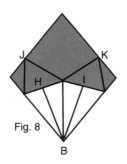

Fig. 8

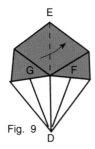

Fig. 9

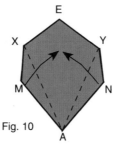

Fig. 10

4. Turn the paper over and repeat step 3 with B as in Fig. 6.

5. Fold along BJ and BK (Fig. 6) so that BH and BI meet at BE (Fig. 7).

6. Open the corners H and I (Fig. 7) so that JH falls on JB and KI falls on KB (Fig. 8).

7. Turn the paper over and repeat steps 5 and 6 (Fig. 9).

8. Fold only the top flap along ED (Fig. 9), and bring G on top of F. Then turn the paper over and bring I on top of H (Fig. 10).

9. Fold along XA and YA (Fig. 10) so that MA and NA meet at EA (Fig. 11).

10. Fold along QR (Fig. 11), bringing point A forward and up (Fig. 12).

11. Fold along OP (Figs. 12 and 13).

12. Turn the paper over and repeat steps 9, 10, and 11 on the other side with corner C, and then with B and D (Fig. 14).

13. Carefully insert your fingers into the candy box and flatten E (Fig. 15).

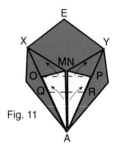

Fig. 11

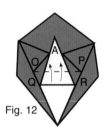

Fig. 12

Fig. 13

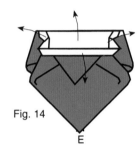

Fig. 14

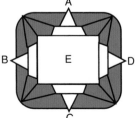

Fig. 15

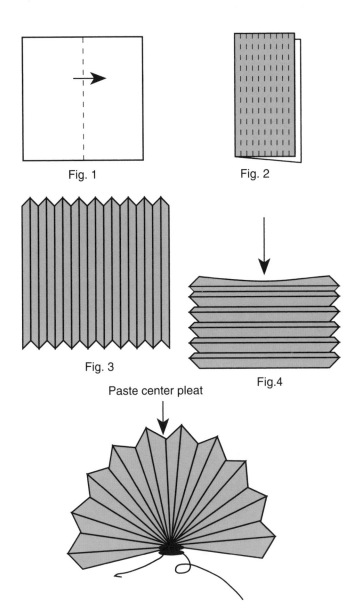

Fig. 1

Fig. 2

Fig. 3

Fig.4

Paste center pleat

Fan

1. Take a square piece of paper and fold in half (Fig. 1). Make lengthwise folds (accordion fashion) across the entire breadth of the paper (Fig. 2) and then open to get Fig. 3.

2. Fold in half as shown in Fig. 4 then paste the center pleats together.

3. To complete, tie a piece of string about one-half inch up from the bottom. See Fig. 5.

Pinwheel

1. Take a square sheet of paper and fold it so that AC and BD (Fig. 1) meet at the center line EF and look like Fig. 2.

2. Fold OM back along the line QR so that OM meets PN. This will result in Fig. 3.

3. Fold along ST so that PN meets QR as in Fig. 4. Note that flap OM remains where it is for the present.

4. Pull out corners D and C as in Fig. 5.

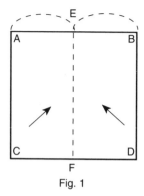

Fig. 1

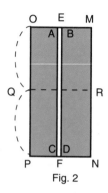

Fig. 2

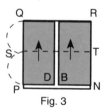

Fig. 3

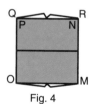

Fig. 4

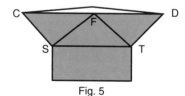

Fig. 5

14

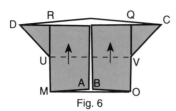

Fig. 6

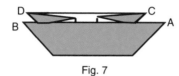

Fig. 7

Fig. 8

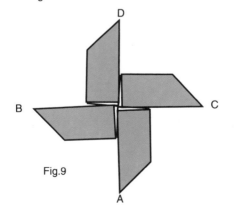

Fig.9

5. Turn the paper over and fold so that MO meets RQ (Fig. 6). Pull out corners A and B and you will get Fig. 7.

6. Spread out Fig. 7 resulting in Fig. 8.

7. Fold corner D upward and corner A downward and you will get Fig. 9.

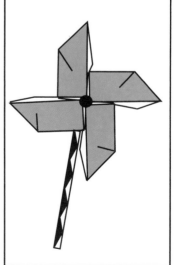

Flowers

1. Fold a square sheet of paper down the middle (Fig. 1) at EF in order to get Fig. 2.

2. Crease in the middle at GH and reopen.

3. Bring the corner F up between D and B so that it meets G, thus placing HF along GH. See Fig. 3. DHB will then form an upside-down triangle.

4. Repeat the step with E (Fig. 4).

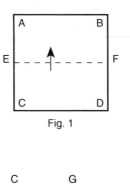

Fig. 1

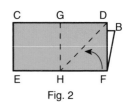

Fig. 2

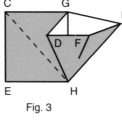

Fig. 3

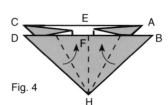

Fig. 4

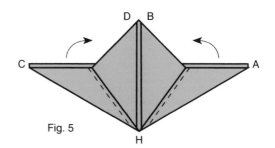

Fig. 5

16

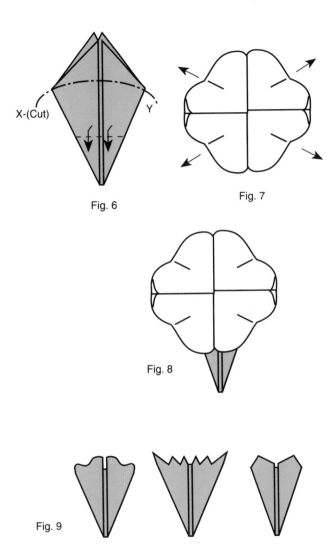

Fig. 6

Fig. 7

Fig. 8

Fig. 9

5. Bring the corners B and D forward to meet at the center over FH as in Fig. 5.

6. Turn the paper over and do the same with corners A and C.

7. Cut off the points with a pair of scissors (Fig. 6).

8. Open the petals, as shown in Fig. 7, as far down as XY and you will get Fig. 8.

9. It is possible to make many kinds of flowers by cutting the petals into various shapes. See Fig. 9.

Helmet

1. Fold a square piece of paper along line BD (Fig. 1) so that corner A is over corner C as shown in Fig. 2.

2. Fold along EF and EG so that corners B and D meet at point A (Fig. 3).

3. Fold up points B and D so that they meet at E as shown in Fig. 4.

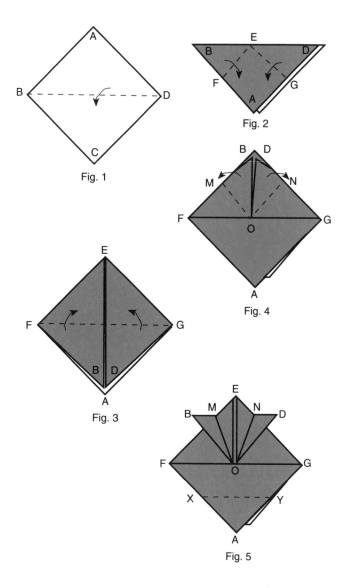

Fig. 1

Fig. 2

Fig. 3

Fig. 4

Fig. 5

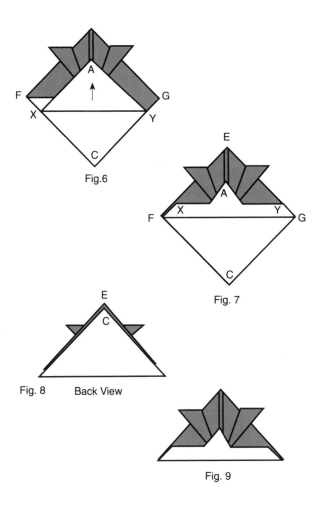

Fig.6

Fig. 7

Fig. 8   Back View

Fig. 9

4. Bring forward point B and fold this flap along OM (Fig. 5). Point M is about one-third of the way down EF.

5. Do the same with point D, folding along ON.

6. Fold at XY (Fig. 6) so that point A is over and above point O.

7. Fold this front flap again at FG to make Fig. 7.

8. Turn over and fold C so it meets E (Fig. 8).

9. Turn over again and the result is Fig. 9.

Jet Plane

1. Fold a square piece of paper along EF (Fig. 1) so that corner B meets center O (Fig. 2).

2. Fold along GH (Fig. 2) so that corner C meets B at center O (Fig. 3).

3. Fold along IJ (Fig. 3) so that edge FD meets CH (Fig. 4).

4. Fold along KI (Fig. 4) so that edge AE meets GC (Fig. 5).

5. Fold along line LNM (Fig. 5) so that D falls on F (Fig. 6).

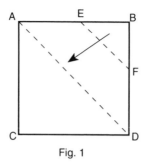

Fig. 1

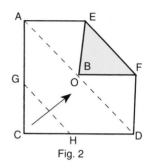

Fig. 2

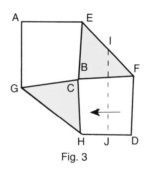

Fig. 3

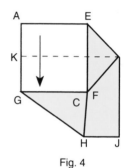

Fig. 4

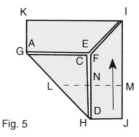

Fig. 5

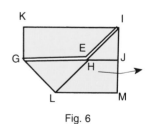

Fig. 6

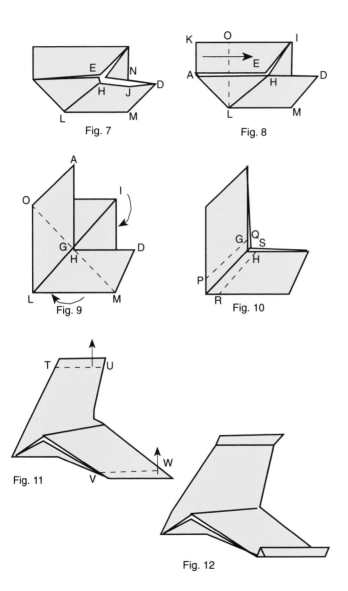

Fig. 7

Fig. 8

Fig. 9

Fig. 10

Fig. 11

Fig. 12

6. Open corner J, bringing corner D to the right, thus making MJ fall on MN (Fig. 7).

7. Repeat steps 5 and 6 with A (Figs. 8 and 9).

8. Fold back I along OM so that corner I falls underneath L (Fig. 9).

9. Fold along PQ and RS so that the two sides touch each other (Fig. 10).

10. Fold along TU and VW (Fig. 11) so that the two edges turn up (Figs. 11 and 12).

21

Kimono

1. Fold a square sheet of paper along line EF (Fig. 1) so AC falls on BD (Fig. 2).

2. Fold forward at GH, about one-quarter of an inch down from EA, and once more at IJ (Figs. 2 and 3).

3. Fold back corners I and J along OM and ON (Fig. 3) so that OI and OJ meet at the center in the back (Fig.4). Point O is halfway between I and J.

4. Fold back point O along PQ and then fold forward along RS so that PQ falls on FC as shown in Figs. 4 and 5.

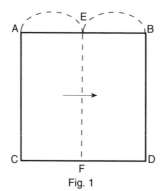

Fig. 1

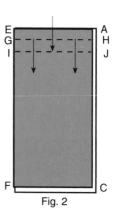

Fig. 2

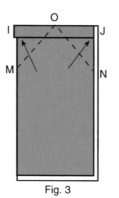

Fig. 3

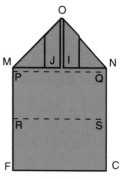

Fig. 4

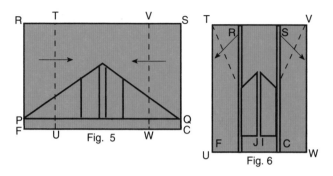

Fig. 5

Fig. 6

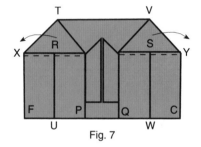

Fig. 7

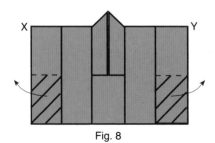

Fig. 8

5. Fold along TU and VW (Fig. 5) so that RF touches collar line J, and SC touches collar line I (Fig. 6).

6. Lift F, separating it from P, and open corner R so that point R falls on TU. Do the same with C and S (Figs. 6 and 7).

7. Fold back along XY (Figs. 7 and 8).

8. To make the sleeves, fold back only the back flap (Fig. 8).

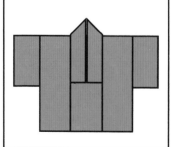

Lantern

1. Crease a square piece of paper as shown in Fig. 1 and then spread open.

2. Fold the four corners A, B, C, and D forward so that they meet at the center as in Figs. 2 and 3.

3. Turn over and fold the four corners E, F, G and H so that they meet at the center as in Fig. 4.

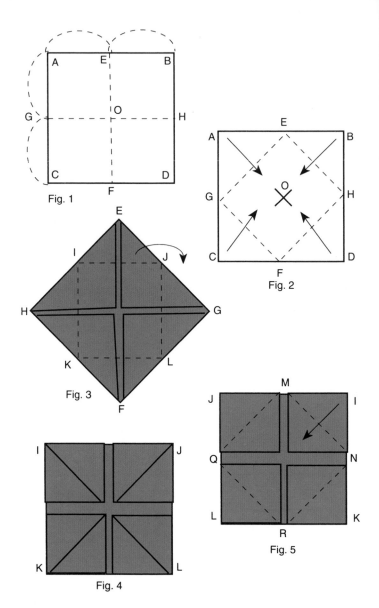

Fig. 1

Fig. 2

Fig. 3

Fig. 4

Fig. 5

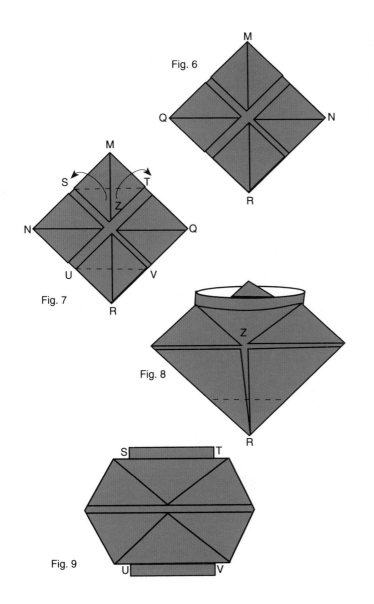

Fig. 6

Fig. 7

Fig. 8

Fig. 9

4. Turn the paper over once more and you will have Fig. 5.

5. Next, fold the corners I, J, K, and L forward once more to meet at the center. Turn the paper over and you will have Fig. 6.

6. Using both thumbs, push open MZ as in Figs. 7 and 8. Do the same with ZR and you will get Fig. 9.

Table

1. Fold a square piece of paper along GH and IJ (Fig. 1) so that edges AC and BD meet at center EF (Fig. 2).

2. Fold GI back along KL (Fig. 2) so that GI will be under HJ (Fig. 3).

3. Fold the top flap along MN (Fig. 3) so that HJ falls on KL (Fig. 4).

4. Make a crease along CM and DN (Fig. 4) and then pull out corners C and D (Fig. 5).

5. Turn the paper over and repeat steps 3 and 4.

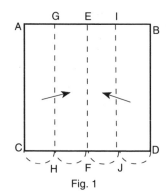

Fig. 1

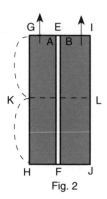

Fig. 2

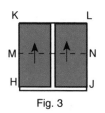

Fig. 3

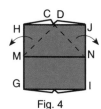

Fig. 4

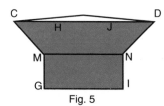

Fig. 5

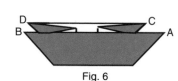

Fig. 6

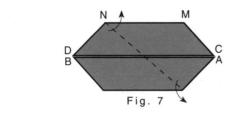

Fig. 7

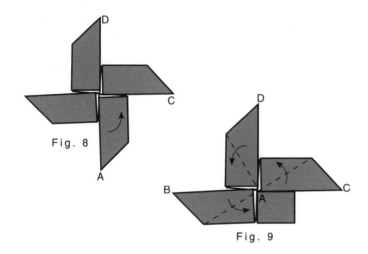

Fig. 8

Fig. 9

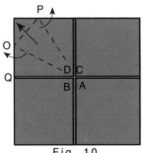

Fig. 10

6. Spread Fig. 6 out so that it looks like Fig. 7.

7. Fold D upward and A downward (Figs. 7 and 8).

8. Open corner A (Fig. 8) and bring point A to the center (Fig. 9).

9. Repeat step 8 at corners B, C, and D (Figs. 9 and 10).

10. Crease at OD and PD (Fig. 10) so that QD and JD meet at the center. Then crease at OP. Lift up D, folding along OP so that Q and J meet at the middle (Fig. 11) on DZ.

11. Repeat step 10 for the other corners A, B, and C (Figs. 11 and 12).

12. Fold along DR and DS (Fig. 12) so that DO meets DP at the center on DZ.

13. Repeat step 12 on corners A, B, and C (Fig. 13).

14. To make the legs stand, fold along TU (Fig. 13).

15. Repeat step 14 on corners C, A, and B (Fig. 14).

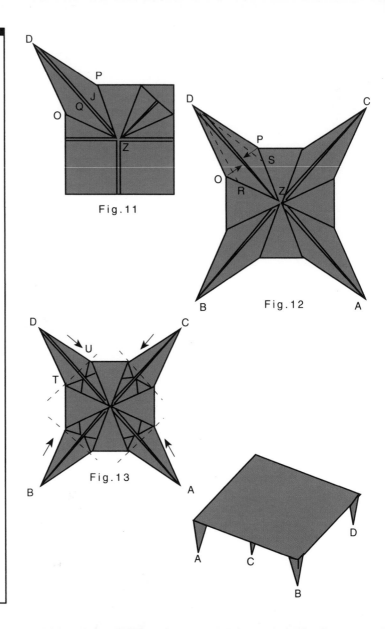

Fig.11

Fig.12

Fig.13

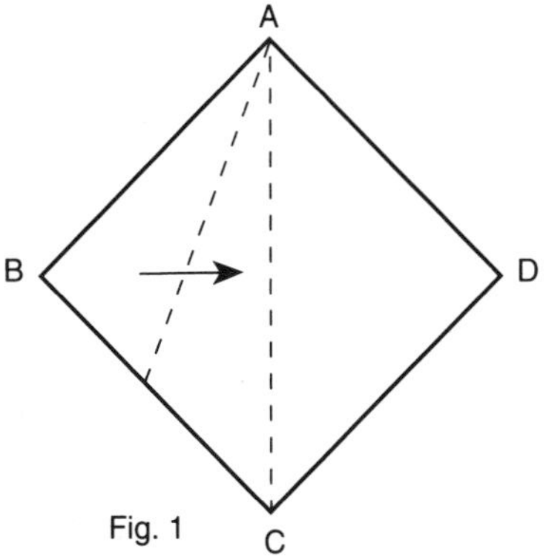

Fig. 1

Fig. 2

Fig. 3

Fig. 4

Fig. 5

Sailboat

1. Take a square piece of paper and fold it along line AC so that point B meets point D. Crease and then re-open as in Fig. 1.

2. Fold AB over to meet the center line AC (Fig. 2).

3. Do the same with AD so as to make Fig. 3.

4. Fold along line MN so that point C is above points B and D. See Fig.4.

5. To complete, fold along line XY so that points M and N look like Fig. 5.

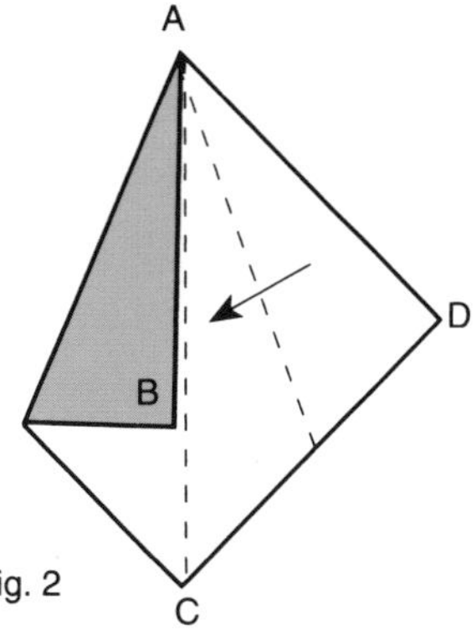

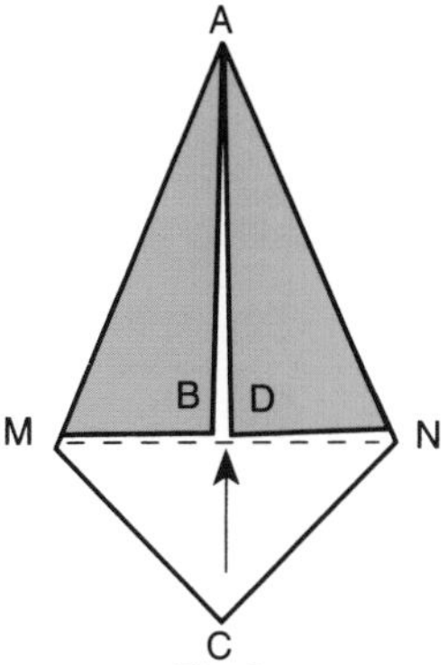

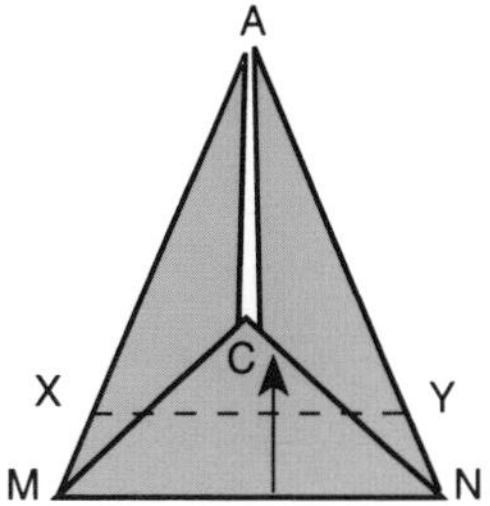

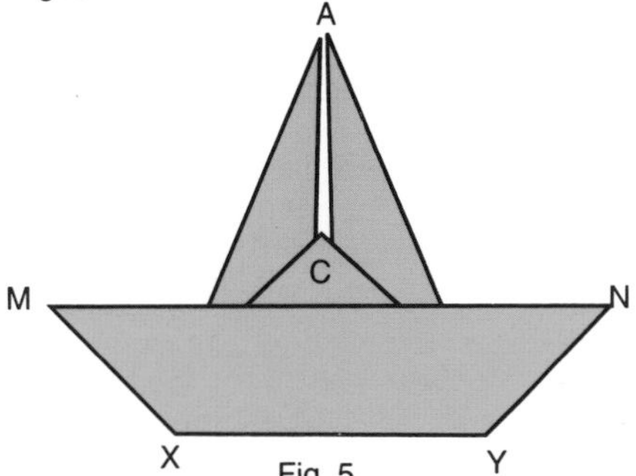

29

Ship

1. Fold a square piece of paper down the center on line EF as shown in Fig. 1, crease, and then unfold.

2. Fold at GH and IJ so that edges AC and BD meet at the center line EF. This results in Fig. 2.

3. Fold at MN so that edge HJ reaches the center line XY, forming Fig. 3.

4. Pull out corners C and D in order to form Fig. 4.

5. Fold backwards at OP so that edge GI is directly under MN as shown in Fig. 5.

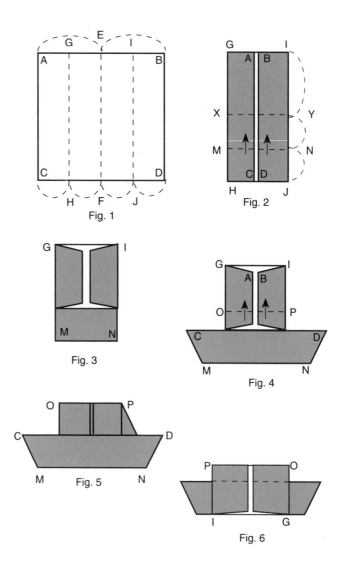

Fig. 1

Fig. 2

Fig. 3

Fig. 4

Fig. 5

Fig. 6

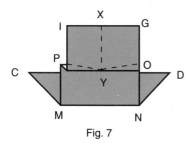

Fig. 7

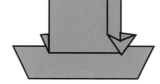

Fig. 8

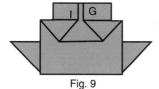

Fig. 9

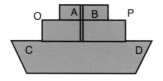

Fig. 10

6. Turn over to get Fig. 6.

7. Fold so that the edge IG is over and above PO as in Fig. 7.

8. Bring point G forward and to the left so that it is directly over X, which is in the center. Fig. 8 shows how this is done. Do the same with point I in order to get Fig. 9.

9. Turn over and you will have the ship shown in Fig. 10.

31

The Tuttle Story:
"Books to Span the East and West"

Most people are surprised to learn that the world's largest publisher of books on Asia had its humble beginnings in the tiny American state of Vermont. The company's founder, Charles E. Tuttle, belonged to a New England family steeped in publishing. And his first love was naturally books—especially old and rare editions.

Immediately after WW II, serving in Tokyo under General Douglas MacArthur, Tuttle was tasked with reviving the Japanese publishing industry. He later founded the Charles E. Tuttle Publishing Company, which still thrives today as one of the world's leading independent publishers.

Though a westerner, Tuttle was hugely instrumental in bringing a knowledge of Japan and Asia to a world hungry for information about the East. By the time of his death in 1993, Tuttle had published over 6,000 books on Asian culture, history and art—a legacy honored by the Japanese emperor with the "Order of the Sacred Treasure," the highest tribute Japan can bestow upon a non-Japanese.

With a backlist of 1,500 titles, Tuttle Publishing is more active today than at any time in its past—inspired by Charles Tuttle's core mission to publish fine books to span the East and West and provide a greater understanding of each.

ORIGAMI FUN

Published by Tuttle Publishing, an imprint of Periplus Editions (HK) Ltd.

www.tuttlepublishing.com

Design by Jean M. Ploss

Published as part of *The Complete Origami Kit*
Not to be sold separately

LCC Card No. 2004558859
ISBN: 978-0-8048-1816-2

Distributed by

North America, Latin America & Europe
Tuttle Publishing
364 Innovation Drive, North Clarendon, VT 05759-9436 U.S.A.
Tel: 1 (802) 773-8930; Fax: 1 (802) 773-6993
info@tuttlepublishing.com   www.tuttlepublishing.com

Japan
Tuttle Publishing
Yaekari Building, 3rd Floor,
5-4-12 Osaki, Shinagawa-ku, Tokyo 141 0032
Tel: (81) 3 5437-0171; Fax: (81) 3 5437-0755
sales@tuttle.co.jp   www.tuttle.co.jp

Asia Pacific
Berkeley Books Pte. Ltd.
61 Tai Seng Avenue #02-12, Singapore 534167
Tel: (65) 6280-1330; Fax: (65) 6280-6290
inquiries@periplus.com.sg   www.periplus.com

16 15 14 13 12   12 11 10 9 8 7   1203EP

Printed in Hong Kong